GOVAN ON THE CLYDE

Patrick Donnelly

GLASGOW CITY LIBRARIES

Govan Burgh Arms

The arms symbolise the ancient and modern industries of the Burgh. In olden times the district was famed for farming, and also for salmon fishing in the Clyde, and these are remembered in the sheaf of wheat crossed by a salmon for crest but the sheaf has been adopted from the Coat of Arms of Mrs. Rowan of Holmfauldhead. The modern industry of shipbuilding is shown in the shield bearing a ship on the stocks. Above are two five-pointed stars or mullets on horizontal lines or azure. These mullets were also taken from the Coat of Arms of Mrs. Rowan. The shield is surmounted by a helmet, and below there is a thistle. The supporters are, on the right hand side a ship-carpenter holding his mallet, and on the left hand side a draughtsman or engineer bearing a plan. The motto 'Nihil sine labore' (Nothing without work), is appropriate.

ISBN 0-906169-41-0
© Glasgow City Libraries 1994
Cover illustration: 'Govan on the Clyde c.1845' by William Simpson
Published by Glasgow City Libraries Publications Board,
The Mitchell Library, North Street, Glasgow G3 7DN
Printed by J. McVicar Printers, Glasgow

INTRODUCTION

This book is a modest contribution to the history and lore of Govan, also known as 'God's Country' and 'Sunny Go-Van', and is intended not only for Govanites (those with Govan connections and proud of them!) but also for anyone interested in local history and reminiscence in general. Condensing a very large collection into a relatively small volume proved impossible, so with advance apologies for any glaring omissions and inaccuracies, here is a rough guide to contents –

Although the material has been included in the section considered most appropriate, many readers' thoughts will no doubt drift as they wander down memory lane. Initial research was based on *The Govan Press* files and T.C.F. Brotchie's *History of Govan*, from both of which illustrations were taken. Many thanks are also due for use of illustrations to the following:-
Glasgow City Libraries and Strathclyde Regional Archives (who between them provided most); People's Palace (p. 63); Mrs. Jane Clements (pp. 33, 56, 59, 62 and 64), Kvaerner (p.22).

I am very grateful to John Nichol, Jean Melville, Bob McClement and Adam McNaughton for poetic contributions and to Archie Fisher for permission to reproduce *The Shipyard Apprentice* and to Mrs. J. McMillan for *The Govan Billiard Hall* respectively, and Margaret Thomson Davis for permission to quote from her novel *The Breadmakers*. Debts of gratitude are also due to Bob McFarlane, Gavin Thomson, Biff Carmichael, John Eaglesham, Moira Thorburn and Margaret McBride. Special thanks to Bill Wilson and to my daughter Elaine Sawicki.

The book is dedicated to the memory of my Ma an' Da – Martha Niblock and Big Pat - two real Govanites.

GOVAN IN 1757.

This sketch shows the Moot Hill and the post-Reformation Church of Govan taken down in 1761–62. The drawing was done from a sketch by Robert Paul. It is dated 1757, and is the earliest known picture of Govan and the only picture showing the ancient Church of the Reformation period, and the much more ancient Moot Hill. Paul's original drawing of this spot measures 6.5 inches long by 4 inches deep. The earliest picture of Govan hitherto published is dated 1815, a fact that emphasises the invaluable character of Paul's drawing.

The Place Name Govan

'Twa myles abone the toune of Renfrou is a gret and ane large village vpon the watir of clyde named Goevan; because it brewis gude ale commended throuch the hail land'. Bishop Leslie 1578.

Based on this statement, some writers have contended that the name is derived from the two Saxon words 'God win' - 'good wine'. However, used throughout history in many forms (e.g. Guvan, Guven, Gwvan, Gowan, Goevan, Gowain, Govand, Goven, Govan – of which the first two are the oldest), the name comes from the Celtic Gowan or Welsh Gofan, signifying 'a smith'. Accordingly Govan is the 'land of the smiths'. The word Govan, as we know it today, was first used in an entry in the minute book of the Govan Weavers Society in 1798 – 'At Govan, the first day of June . . .' Previous references had been to Meikle /Mekle Govan or Meilegovan (Meikle, or large, was used to distinguish it from Litil Govan, a hamlet to the east near Stockwell Bridge).

Brief History

Govan's humble origins have been traced to pre-Christian days, although its popular history begins around 565AD, when St. Constantine founded his monastery on the site of the present Govan Old Parish Church. (Inside the main gateway stands a replica of the Govan Cross, and the staff of the original Cross is kept behind the pulpit in the Church). The next significant account is around 1147-53 when King David I, in restoring the fallen bishopric of Glasgow, embraced Govan and Partick within its bounds, including the 'islands between Guven and Perteye or Perthec.' Since it was also about this time that Govan was made a prebend (associated church) of Glasgow Cathedral, this explains why the parish extended over both sides of the river.

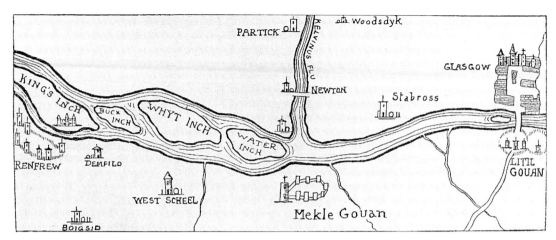

BLAEU'S 1654 map of the islands between Govan and Partick indicates the narrowness and shallowness of the river.

For the next 400 years or so, since the church was the mainspring of the community, references were mostly to ecclesiastical affairs, as Govan remained a veritable sleepy hollow, whose main industries were agriculture and salmon fishing – although by the 16th century there were extensive coal mine workings around Craigton and Drumoyne. The village grew, new trades and crafts, such as weaving, pottery and agriculture, were established, but by 1793, when the population comprised 224 families (1,000 persons), the staple industries still dominated – particularly so in the rich farm-lands of Langlands, Broomloan, Southcroft, Langshot, Drumoyne, Holmfauldhead and Greenfield (some of the district's streets, drives and roads have been named after these lands). Dr. Pollok, in the *Statistical Account of Scotland* (Govan 1795), remarked that 'there is perhaps no parish in the West of Scotland where agriculture is better understood or has been carried out to greater perfection than in Govan'.

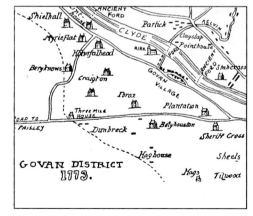

6

DRAWING the salmon nets. c. 1815.

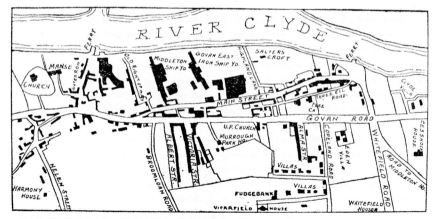

MAP OF GOVAN c. 1858. Whitefield Road to Harmony Row.

By the early part of the 19th century, Govan was rapidly losing its rural aspect, gradually assuming the character of a town as other industries such as Reid's Dye Works near Water Row (motto: 'we live to dye, we dye to live') and Pollok's Silk Mill began to spring up. Above all else, with the deepening of the Clyde from 1759, removal of the islands, and the building of quays and docks, shipbuilding accelerated this change, so that by 1860 the 'new' Govan was in full swing. It soon became obvious that a proper administration was required and the village was created a Burgh from 6th June 1864 under the General Police (Scotland) Act of 1862. With Morris Pollok as its first Lord Provost, the Burgh Commissioners, who had replaced the former village representatives, ensured that over the next 48 years Govan became as well equipped for municipal, social, educational, religious, industrial and general civic purposes as any town in Scotland.

Annexation; or 'The Spider and the Fly'

1868. The good ship Govan had hardly set sail when Glasgow proposed that the Burgh (purely for Parliamentary Boundary purposes!) should come within one of the areas to be represented by the City's three MPs. However, the astute 'toon councillors', well aware of Govan's growing prosperity and stature, as well as the implications of City Taxation, vowed to ward off this veiled threat to their independence. After a strenuous fight, Glasgow was defeated, leaving Govan as part of the Lanarkshire Parliamentary Division.

1870. Glasgow promoted its first Bill in Parliament (for annexation of the Burghs of Govan, Partick, Hillhead and Maryhill) but was sent packing at the second Commons reading – its proposals being considered too sweeping and unreasonable.

1883/4. More 'conjuring tricks' (this time clauses and amendments to existing legislation) proved unsuccessful as Parliament reaffirmed that no community could be annexed against its will. Interestingly, Govan was made a Parliamentary Division in 1884 and remains a constituency despite periodic attempts to rename it (the 1981 proposal to call it Bellahouston would, if successful, have been as calamitous as annexation itself!)

1887/91. The 'werewolf was still peerin' o'er the dyke'. The Boundaries Commission of 1887/8, conceded generally to Glasgow's desires and another Bill was introduced in 1889, leading to the struggles of 1890/1 – which resulted, once more, in Parliamentary support for Govan's cause.

1912. The sinking of the Titanic – and Govan. Local poet John Murray had several years earlier warned of Glasgow's growing desperation:–

'Oor great big sister's in a mess.
Her population's getting less.
If I read richt the public press
She's getting mixed (upset)
And on oor burgh naething less
Her e'e is fixed.'

and so, with Parliamentary approval, Glasgow 'swallowed up' the unwilling Govan. 48 years of independence ended on 5th November 1912, and as the all too short days of wine and roses drew to a close, Govanites had to accept that 'we are not now a community of our own'. Feelings of lost identity and of betrayal, bitterness and resentment, against their own trusted leaders, as well as Glasgow, lasted many a long day – indeed, for some, right down to the present time.

What Happened to Govan's Industries?

During the second half of the 19th century, the former principal industries of salmon fishing, hand loom weaving, silk making, pottery and farming were either gone (many farmers moved to Ayrshire) or fast disappearing, as Govan's fame and prosperity became firmly based on shipbuilding, marine engineering production, heavy engineering and allied industries. The names associated with the rise of Govan shipbuilding were:– McArthur & Alexander (1840), Napier (1842), Smith & Rogers (1843), G. & I. Thomson (1888) and the 'Big Three' – Stephens (1868), Fairfield (see p. 22) and Harland & Wolff (1912). Employment covered nearly every branch of iron and metal trades, and included bridge girder building; bolt, rivet, tube and boiler-making; iron and brass founding; lead pipe and sheet making; coppersmithing; crane building; railway plant and chain making.

Brotchie's tribute to industrial Govan was most appropriate when he wrote of 'one of the great workshops of the world. Within its boundaries, it is impossible to get beyond the sound of the hammer. From early morn till late at night we hear the continuous hum of industry – telling us of the spirited policy of business administration which directs the helms of the burgh's affairs'. This was still the position in 1918, although by then specialisation in passenger liners made the ship-building industry increasingly vulnerable to fluctuations in world demand. Engineering and the other allied industries also suffered as gradually the number of Clyde yards was reduced, with the workforce falling from 43,000 in 1919 to 29,000 in 1930 and much lower to 16,000 during the Depression. In spite of artificially high employment during World War II, the decline of shipbuilding continued with a series of amalgamations and closures, so that by the early 1970s, Clydeside unemployment was well above the national average. Govan's famous yards were all but gone – leaving, after the demise of Upper Clyde Shipbuilders, only Govan Shipbuilders (now Kvaerner). So, although the reversal of Govan's industrial fortunes followed a similar pattern to other areas, the biggest contributory factor was the decline of shipbuilding and associated industries. Sir Murray Stephen confidently predicted in his address to the 1950 AGM of the Govan Weavers Society that 'shipbuilding will not follow the same fate as weaving'. Certainly, all these years on, the industry survives – if only just.

Amongst the 'weel kent' victims of the demise of the old industrial Govan, in addition to firms identifiable on p. 9, were:– most of the SCWS works complex at Shieldhall, Christies Wire Works, The Clyde Foundry, Gourock Rope Works and Thermotank.

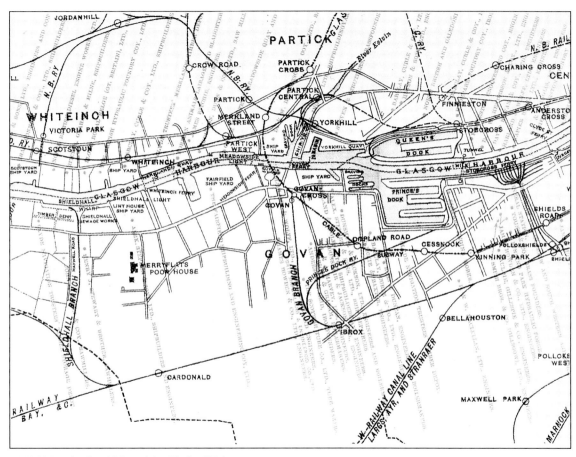

REID'S Navigational Map of the Clyde. 1926.

AERIAL VIEW of river, church, tenements. c. 1935.

Some of the streets in and around this area: Langlands Rd, Sharp St, Dunvegan St, Wanlock St, McKechnie St, Wardrop St, Rathlin St, Howat St, Luath St, Taransay St, Harmony Row, Shaw St, Rosneath St, Nethan St, Logie St, Golspie St, Fairfield St, Garmouth St, Elderpark St, Harhill St.

Whilst the population of Govan rose dramatically, from 9,000 in 1864 to 91,000 in 1904, due to industrial growth, its steady fall, to around 35,000 in the mid 1950s, is not attributable solely to industrial decline. Further explanation lies in successive policies, mostly those of Glasgow Corporation, concerning Govan's housing.

The very rapid expansion of shipbuilding had left the district with a population well in excess of house accommodation, and overcrowding was extraordinary. The Burgh's solution, particularly as workers had to live near their places of employment, was to convert country loans, green fields and farmlands into the tenement lands of what most Govanites of today regard as Old Govan (Govan typified the traditional tenemental way of life in working class areas, and many generations of families spent their entire lives there, normally 'flittin'' through various combinations of houses, closes, streets and roads – the last Friday in May was 'flittin' day' – in what was certainly a close-knit community! Its 'better end' was considered to be at Elder Park, Drumoyne and Linthouse, the last named being called 'The Garden of Eden' because it was 'dry' and therefore a much more righteous area! Although Govan was, by and large, a simple law-abiding community, there were nonetheless some problem families – delinquency and gangs providing minor irritations for the authorities and for fellow Govanites. The street with the worst reputation for drunks, fighting, rent avoidance etc., – with apologies to certain closes in Hoey St, Burndyke St, Elphinstone St, McLean St, Blackburn St, Plantation St and Eaglesham St – was Nethan St, which, from its not inconsiderable ranks of anti-social residents, had produced such gangs as the 'Kellybo', a particularly vicious outfit, the 'Death Valley' and 'Death or Glory Boys' of the 1920s and 30s, as well as the 'Bingoes' and 'Neds' of the '50s).

As far back as 1795, the *Statistical Account* had revealed that the homes of the village were 'old, ill-aired and incommodious', a comment equally applicable to much of Govan's housing stock of the 1920s and 30s which was then in a sorry state through shortages, overcrowding, neglect and deterioration.

New housing, particularly at Drumoyne, Greenhead, Linthouse, Shieldhall, Brighton St, Ibrox, Teucharhill, Mosspark and 'Wine Alley' (officially Broomloan Rd/Moorepark Hill but eventually so called for obvious reasons) enabled many families to stay in the district, but the allocation of houses in these 'Promised Lands' caused quite a 'stooshie' – especially with 'Wine Alley' in the 1930s when it was discovered, as with the Orkney St development of the 1950s, that amongst the new tenants would be incomers, in this case, from Gorbals, Hutchesontown and Anderston!

Further afield, but of the greatest significance and consequence to the people of Govan, as the authorities sought an answer to the critical housing problem, was the building during the years 1934–52 of the schemes at Old Pollok and Craigbank (superior!), Penilee, Nitshill, Priesthill, Househillwood and South Pollok. The biggest exodus to these 'brave new worlds' took place from 1946–58 as 3,000 families, or 12,000–15,000 people, were relocated, most with considerable reluctance and sadness. The feelings of the vast majority about leaving the old burgh were summed up by a local councillor: 'They don't want to live in Pollok. Govan people would like home again. They want back to the district from which they came . . . near to their work and their life-long friends. This can be done by pulling down the old houses and building on the site'.

Most of them stayed, initially by necessity, in the districts which have since, in themselves, produced generations of those migrant Govanites. Not everyone went to the schemes mentioned of course. Many remained in Govan, or went to other areas such as Drumchapel, Easterhouse, or Castlemilk, others emigrated, keeping in touch through *The Press*, or moved to other parts of the country. But for everyone, Govan remained the common bond.

Ahcumfaegovan, ur dae ah? – Govan's Boundaries.

The old saying 'When Govan was Govan' is probably better rearranged as 'When was Govan Govan?', since the only certainty regarding this historically thorny subject is that there will never be complete agreement on exactly what constituted its boundaries. However, the following guidance is offered to assist any relevant discussion, debate or study. (A magnifying glass may come in particularly handy for reading the map!)

Govan Parish. The former parish, which originated in the 12th century, covered a considerable area on both banks of the Clyde. The boundary line followed the River Kelvin to Maryhill in the north, and included Whiteinch, Partick, Dowanhill, Hillhead (including Glasgow University) and Kelvinside. To the south, it embraced the districts of Govan, Ibrox, Plantation, Kinning Park, Tradeston, Laurieston, Gorbals (which became its own parish in 1771 – except under Poor Law legislation), Govanhill, East and West Pollokshields, Strathbungo and Dumbreck. It extended from Jenny's Burn at Polmadie in the east to Dean Park of Renfrew in the west. The parish ceased to exist as such under the 1918 Education (Scotland) Act. Although the Parish Council continued to function for many years – particularly in the administration of Poor Relief.

Govan Burgh 1864–1912. From 1864 to 1901 when Linthouse, represented on the illustration by cross lines, was (willingly!) added, the boundary ran from just beyond Paisley Road Toll in the east to the end of Elder Park in the west at, but excluding, Drive Road.

1912 – At annexation, the Burgh was reconstituted as Wards 27 (Plantation), 28 (Ibrox), 29 (Govan Central) and 30 (Fairfield) of Glasgow, the area to the west of Linthouse being newly added. Further re-alignment came in 1920 with Plantation becoming part of Ward 28 (Kinning Park), Ibrox becoming part of Ward 29 (Govan) and the remainder being Ward 30 (Fairfield). Since World War II, there have been some minor adjustments.

'Govan stoaped at the Toon Hall.'
'Govan finished at Lorne School.'
'Plantation wiz never in Govan.'
'Drumoyne's no Govan, izit?'

Such personal opinions and assertions, based partly on fact and information, but mostly on tradition, family background, attitudes, pride and prejudice, which no amount of persuasion can alter, are particularly common in older Govanites and tend to override official definitions:–

Q : 'Ur yiz baith fae Govan?'
A : 'Naw, ah um – he's fae Linthoose!'.

So – yi pays yir money . . .

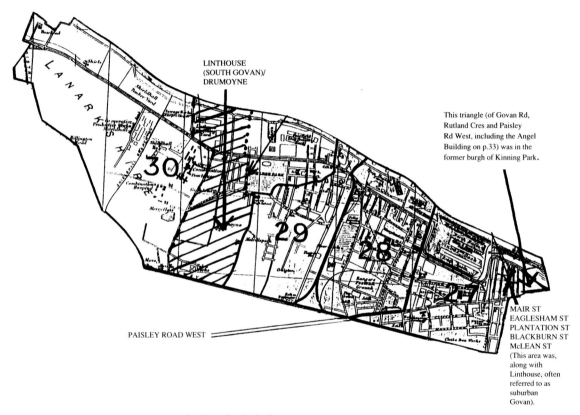

LINTHOUSE
(SOUTH GOVAN)/
DRUMOYNE

This triangle (of Govan Rd,
Rutland Cres and Paisley
Rd West, including the Angel
Building on p.33) was in the
former burgh of Kinning Park.

MAIR ST
EAGLESHAM ST
PLANTATION ST
BLACKBURN ST
McLEAN ST
(This area was,
along with
Linthouse, often
referred to as
suburban
Govan).

PAISLEY ROAD WEST

. . . and yi takes yir choice!

GOOD GOD IN GOVAN! Govan Old Parish Church. c. 1930.

Built, 1884–8, on the site of St. Constantine's monastery, the present location is the fifth since 1136. To the right were Harland & Wolff's platers sheds.

For centuries, with no proper police force till 1864, the Kirk had a difficult office to fulfil as director of the life of the citizens and custodian of their behaviour. To assist them, the elders were empowered to 'pick out men who were prudent and zealous and blameless'. 17th century Session Records tell us that among the misdemeanours regularly dealt with were 'lack of church going, infidelity, disregard of church vows, thoughtless attitude of parents towards baptism, breaking of the Sabbath, illicit traffic in drink, spending undue time in change houses and other places in acts of lousness (looseness) and ungodliness'. O ye of little faith!

WAVERLEY INN, Water Row. 1861. Originally the 16th century 'Ferrie Bot Inn' or 'Buc'.

The licence was transferred around 1900 to Langlands Rd by Mrs. Buchanan, a descendant of the landlord from whom the inn at the ferry derived the name 'Buc'.

It is a strange and ironic fact that in the 17th century, when Govan was becoming more populous and agriculturally developed, the two central points were the Kirk and a hostelry, separated by the graveyard into which revellers frequently spilled! There is further irony in that many of the erstwhile elders and innkeepers have down the centuries been buried in that same graveyard. That relationships were somewhat strained can be seen from this 1651 Kirk Session enactment: 'Whaever shall sell drink to drunken folks shall come under the same censure as drunkards. As shall also who keep drunkards on their premises or fills drink to any save in cases of necessitee up till ten hour at evin'.

THE OLD (SILK) MILL BY THE STREAM. Engraving by J. Swan. 1824.

Established in that year by Morris Pollok, on the ground later taken over by the east (Linthouse) end of Fairfields Yard, this was the first factory for throwing silk in Scotland and an early example of Industrial Age Govan. It was also one of the first factories heated and ventilated by steam so that, although hours were long (grown ups – 11 hrs per day; children 10–11 hrs) and wages poor (2 shillings – 18 shillings a week) working conditions were considered reasonable.
Even after the industry declined, the Factory remained a landmark for paddle steamer travellers, until its removal in 1901.

THE SHIPYARD APPRENTICE

I was born in the shadow of a Fairfield crane, and the blast of a freighter's horn,
Was the very first sound that reached my ears, on the morning I was born,
I lay and listened to the shipyard noise coming out of the great unknown,
And was sung to sleep by the mother tongue, that was to be my own.

But before I grew to one year old, I heard the sirens scream
As a city watched in the blacked out night a wandering searchlight beam.
And then at last I woke and rose, to my first day of peace
But I'd learned that the battle to stay alive was never going to cease.

For I've sat and I've listened to my father tell, of the days that he once knew
When you either sweated for a measly wage, or you joined the parish queue
And as times grew harder day by day along the riverside
I oftimes heard my mother say 'It was tears that made the Clyde'.

I've sat in the school from nine to four, and I've dreamed of the world outside
Where the riveter and the plater watch their ships slip to the Clyde
I've served my time behind shipyard gates, and I sometimes mourn my lot
But if any man tries to mess me about, I'll fight as my father fought.

(Archie Fisher).

'It's three yerds fae Linthoose tae Govan – Stevies, Fairfields and Harlands'

Alexander Stephen & Sons Ltd (Linthouse 1868-c.1970) built a great variety of vessels including a number of notable sailing ships (the 4 masted barque 'Carradale', seen here, was one of the last in 1889 and epitomises Govan's romantic link with the sea). Steamers, including cargo and passenger vessels followed. Among the former were their chilled fruit carriers – especially those for the banana trade belonging to Elder and Fyffe (hence the saying 'Dae ye think ah came up the Clyde oan a banana boat?'). Passenger ships (for the Anchor Line, P&O, and British India), fast minelayers and destroyers and an aircraft carrier were built.

THE FAIRFIELD FLEET. 1907.

Fairfield Shipbuilding and Engineering Co. Ltd.
Established in 1834 as an engineering business, it became Randolph, Elder & Co. in 1852, John Elder & Co. in 1868 and Fairfield & Co. in 1885. Now Kvaerner.

Designed to build large ships (cargo, Cunard and other passenger liners) the yard also constructed many war vessels for the Admiralty, including sloops, destroyers, cruisers, battleships and aircraft carriers. This photograph contrasts sharply with that on the previous page, and shows another, developing, aspect of Govan shipbuilding in the late 19th and early 20th centuries.

HARLAND & WOLFF (BELFAST) LTD. 1923.

Seen here in the foreground, this was the 'youngest' of the three great modern Govan yards and the one with the shortest life span (1912–1962). Recruiting mainly from Northern Irish people, many of whom were housed in the tenements near the yard, Harlands built many important vessels, although most of its high prestige contracts went to Belfast, construction was mainly of cargo vessels with a few passenger ships and Admiralty contracts.

CROWD AT FAIRFIELD. c. 1910.

'The responsibility of the Clyde is great. The British Empire is looking to the Clyde, France is looking to the Clyde, the democracies of the world are looking to the Clyde, and I am sure they will not look in vain'. Lloyd George 1917.
Nor did they as the world-wide reputation of Clyde Shipbuilding proved. The scene shows some of the men who ensured, by their skill and endeavour, Govan's lasting fame.

The Immigrant Govanite

Govan's substantial Irish population were overwhelmingly Catholic. Having fled the famines of the 1840s in great numbers, they encountered hostility from the Scottish Protestant majority and discrimination in the various trades, and so withdrew into their own communities. There, the key influence was the Catholic Church and, as most Irish neighbourhoods were organised around the parish and its church, priests became important, powerful figures. St. Anthony's (opposite) was the first such church in 1864, followed by St. Saviour's (1897) and St. Constantine's (1921).

Highlanders had been in Govan long before the Irish, albeit in much smaller numbers, and although more readily accepted, largely due to their Scottish identity, had nevertheless fallen foul of the Kirk Session which in 1659 organised a petition for removing 'those heilandmen in the toune' who did not quite practice the order of the court.

GOVAN IRISH CLUB. c. 1910.

One of the clubs where the Irish met to pursue their own social and political ends. Entrance was via the pend of this 1830s building in Neptune St (formerly Victoria St and known as the Irish Channel). Next to the pend is a haberdashery and McGinty's Ham & Egg Store.

The rise of the Labour Party was an important event for the entire Irish community in Govan providing working class Protestants and Catholics with the opportunity to identify with a political party which stressed the common bond of social, political and economic grievances.

Educating the Masses

OLD PARISH SCHOOL, at the Cross. c.1910. Built 1788–1800.

The *Statistical Account of Scotland* (1795) found that Govan's children had 'been neglected in their education' and, by the mid-nineteenth century, the provision of educational facilities for a rapidly growing population had become a major problem. Improvement came through the Govan Parish School Board (1873–1918) which came to be considered the most progressive in Scotland – building 34 new schools, and providing medical inspection, swimming baths, and education for the handicapped.

N.B. The education area was the Parish, not the Burgh. The words GOVAN PARISH SCHOOL BOARD can still be seen in surviving school buildings e.g. Whiteinch, Hyndland, Broomhill, Partick.

ELDER FREE PUBLIC LIBRARY. 228a Langlands Rd. 1903.

'I should like to say to the workers in Govan that Mrs. Elder had you chiefly in mind when she donated funds for this living monument with a soul in it. I trust this may not be forgotten by you'. (Andrew Carnegie on officially opening the library in 1903).

The Govan Library as it became known locally, certainly wasn't forgotten, especially by generations of self-educated Govanites who availed themselves of its Reading Room and magnificent collection of books. The oldest general public library in Glasgow, it features amongst its local history material, a set of the *Govan Press* from 1878–1986.

WHEN CONSTABULARY DUTY'S TO BE DONE . . . 1901.

Govan's first Police Force of 1864 comprised a superintendent and ten constables, which (necessarily!) expanded, in proportion to the population growth, to a chief constable, four lieutenants, eleven sergeants and 95 constables by 1905. Orkney St and the 'Poalis Oafis' were to become almost synonymous, and the Court was at times a great source of entertainment and amusement. As in the case of one Thomas McLuskey who, as reported in the *Press*, was convicted of 'consigning all the Protestants within hearing to the baleful shadows of Hades', sentenced to 14 days in prison and fined 7s 6d. On his release, he immediately went to the Court demanding to see 'the magistrate that tried me' and, on being asked why, replied 'Ah've done ma 14 days, noo ah want ma seven an' six'.

READ ALL ABOUT IT! Cossar's Kingdom. c.1910.

John Cossar printed and distributed the town's first newspaper, *The Govan Chronicle* on Saturday, 22 May 1875, and in 1878 established from here *The Govan Press*. Issued every Friday, including war years, for over a century (the firm moved premises and closed in 1983), the paper was very popular at home and abroad. Friday night was *Press* night! The busts in the illustration are l. to r.:– Gutenberg, Scott, Mr. & Mrs. Cossar, Burns and Caxton.

Also seen is 'Coffee Joe's' working men's tavern – open from 7 a.m. and used mainly by workers from the dry docks. Trade suffered as unemployment rose and latterly schoolchildren were allowed in (it closed in the mid 60s).

KITTLE CORNER, corner of Shaw St and Govan Rd. c. 1890.

The Scots word 'kittle' has several meanings and was originally used locally to describe this particularly windy and awkward corner. Perhaps 'to warm up and show life in speaking' would be more appropriate, since this was also a favourite meeting-place in the days before 'the steamie'. The passing of this romantic aspect of Old Govan towards the end of the 19th Century, was much lamented by Brotchie:– 'A densely populated industrial town has taken the place of the ancient village and well nigh obliterates every trace of it. Of theekit houses, once upon a time a feature of rural Govan, a few linger on. The searcher in the bye-ways of the modern burgh will light upon one or two buried in the midst of tall and sober coloured tenements whose raking height and barrack like structures carefully prevent a glimpse of sunshine cheering the oldeworlde cottage with its warmth'.

'Oh, Where is the Govan that I used to know?' by John Nichol
(Tune: 'The Old Orange Flute')

Chorus: Tra-la-la, Tra-la-lee. Oh, where is the Govan that once used to be

Oh, where is the Govan that I used to know?
Walkers and Irwins, The Poly, the Co.,
The walk doon the Gaulley each Saturday night,
Wi' the Salvation Army, sae cheerie and bright.

The sail on the Ferry, the hurl oan the caur,
For just a few coppers you'd go pretty faur,
Tae 'Mulguy', or Airdrie, and Gleniffer too,
And the Tramway officials were pleasant tae you!

Each Saturday noontime, the kiddies would yell,
When they heard the first wailing o' 'Elders Farewell',
Then they'd rush tae their sweetshops, and there they
would stey,
Tae their da came along, and he haunt them their pey!

Tae play in the Bella a' day, we were fond,
Or we paddled and fished, in oor ain Elder's pond,
And we climbed the high dykes, where we dared one and a',
Got the fright o' oor life, when we fell aff the wa'.

The first Friday in June we a' had a great terr,
For that was the night o' the Old Govan Fair,
Patsy Scanlan, Jimsey Reynolds and others beside,
Had us howling we' laughter, or bursting wi' pride.

T'wards the end o' the week, when the money was
gone,
Oor boots and oor shoes took a walk tae the pawn,
Wi' some cash in their pockets, they felt like a swell,
And some of them selt their pawn tickets as well.

The yerds by the river, stood thick, side by side
The hammer's ding-dong was the song o' the Clyde,
Each Street had its shops and its pubs and a pawn,
So each Friday night there was some carry on.

They got rid o' the caurs; then the ferries went too!
They shut a' the yairds, put the men on the 'Broo',
Still they promised Utopia – but I don't think that's true,
It will no be the Govan that we a' once knew.

PAISLEY ROAD TOLL AND THE
ANGEL BUILDING. c. 1890.

'The Gateway to Govan' and the start of a casual
stroll through the Govan of living memory. This
particular angel, although considered by many
Govanites to be part of their territory, did not spread
her wings in 'God's Country', but in Kinning Park.

On the left is one of the horse-drawn trams which
plied between the Toll and Ibrox. To the right is a
steam tram bound for Fairfields Yard.

AT PRINCES DOCK. c. 1955.

This stretch of Govan Road, from the Tram Depot at Lorne St to the Town Hall at Summertown Road, was known as the 'ten miler', because it seemed such a long walk unbroken by side streets. This was part of a favourite stroll to and from Glasgow, but was considered by some to be 'ootside' Govan (see also pp.14–15).
Govan had one of the busiest tram highways in Glasgow – particularly due to workers in the yards and football supporters (Ibrox, Tinto and Moore Parks).

Municipal Buildings, Govan

CORRIDORS OF POWER, Municipal Buildings. c. 1905.

It was not until 1901 that Govan was provided with a Town Hall and Municipal Buildings in keeping with its status as the fifth largest Police Burgh in Scotland. Previously, affairs had been run from the Old Govan Hall in Robert St and later from the Burgh Hall in Orkney St (now the Police Station). Thousands of functions, meetings, rallies etc. were held down the years, and it was also here, at the 'Towny' dancing, that many a lad met his lass – and his downfall? To the left, in Summertown Rd, was the office where the parish poor received handouts. Opposite this were Green's Picturedrome and the boxing booths where Primo Carnera, world heavyweight boxing champion in the '30s, once fought an exhibition bout.

443 GOVAN ROAD, corner of Elphinstone St. c. 1930.

'There is no baker in the place, no butcher and no public market of any kind. All sorts of provisions, therefore, excepting meal and potatoes, cost the inhabitants more than if they lived in Glasgow because they must go thither to purchase them'. *Statistical Account of Scotland* – 1795.

As time went by matters improved. Tenement corner shops were numerous and made shopping easier for weary 'mithers' – many with 'squads o' weans'. In his 1959 study, *Reshaping a City*, T. Brennan found that in Govan 'men are rarely seen in food shops, are never seen wheeling a pram, and would look ridiculous if they had to carry home a bunch of flowers!' He wasn't contradicted!

GOVAN ROAD, looking west to the Cross. 1890.

The street lamp in the foreground shows the turn in Govan Rd at the Whitefield Bar. The first opening on the left is Carmichael St (Arthur Mone's was the corner pub) and on the next corner (Copland Rd) was, in contrast to Mone's, St.Columba's Gaelic Church. Further down were Hoey St and Burndyke St – street bookies' territory! Opposite Copland Rd, was the Three Ell Lane (so called because it equalled in width three weaver's ells) from the bottom of which sailed the Yorkhill ferry. Further down was the Napier Old Model Lodging Housing at Clydebrae St.

MILLER'S CORNER. Orkney St. c. 1935.

Judging from this letter of complaint to the *Press*, Govan's tenement dwellers pursued some interesting pastimes for which the buildings were not, one would assume, originally intended –

'Will any of your readers kindly inform me . . . if there is any law in existence to prevent the . . . horrible practice of stairhead courting which is being carried out to extreme. I am already aware of the Act for loitering in closes, lanes, etc. but the difference between that and a couple far up in each other's arms is very great'. Pity the actual tenements in question were not specified!

GOVAN ROAD, looking to the Cross from Orkney St. 1930.

Dominating this scene is the Harland & Wolff platers shed, next to which is the Continental ice-cream shop and Tony the Barber's. Also in and around this Neptune St/Orkney St/Broomloan Rd area are – the Police and Fire Stations, City Wireless, Mary O'Hara's rag store, the Potted Heid Bank, and Buchanan's Bakery (whose cheaper unsliced bread was long preferred by many!)

THE PLAZA, Govan Cross. 1953. 'We are the boys and girls well known as . . . the minors of the ABC'.

Govanites were cinema mad – graduation to the 'big pictures' being via the Plaza Minors' Club on Saturday mornings. Other cinemas round and about were:- The Lyceum (corner of Govan Rd/McKechnie St 1939); Elder, or 'flea pit' (Rathlin St 1916); Vogue (opp. South Govan Town Hall 1939); Aldwych (Cardonald 1939, later the Vogue, now Safeway); Westway (Cardonald 1934, later the Flamingo Ballroom, or the 'Flam', and now Bingo); Mosspark (Paisley Rd West 1924, now DSS Offices); Capitol (Lorne St); Lorne and the Imperial (Paisley Rd Toll 1920, now Grand Old Opry). Cinema City (Glasgow) eat your heart out!

THE CROSS. GOVAN

GOVAN CROSS. 'Centre of the known universe'. c. 1910.

The Square, described in 1910, somewhat disapprovingly, as 'the rendezvous of the patent medicine man and the itinerant preacher', was to become Govan's own Hyde Park Corner, particularly in the 1930s. As there was always great interest in political, social and religious matters, crowds thronged to hear local orators and debaters tackle the burning issues of the day.

GREENHAUGH STREET. 1933.

From left to right in the previous illustration:–
Govan Tramways Depot (Greenhaugh St/Robert St became the terminus for buses to the housing schemes and Hillington Industrial Estate); the Rosshire Bar ('The Hielanman's'); Subway (which provided a somewhat noisy lullaby for tenement dwellers); the Boilermakers Hall; Watson's Bar ('Staunin-up Boab's'); and McEwans Newsagents (also a removal firm). Long Subway queues, mostly of shipyard workers, were a common sight, round into the Govan Road, past the Govan Arms, Millers and into Helen St at Irwins (passing trade in the various hostelries was reported to be brisk at such times!).

THE SINGER AT THE SUBWAY

In rain or shine you'd see him there, this puir auld sightless man
Jist ootside the subway station, wi' a tinny in his han'.
He wisnae nae Caruso, him, notes werenae low an' sweet
Yet there were many who stopped tae hear this auld singer in the street.

There were folks who'd pass him by, wi' just a thankless shrug
But ah jist loved tae hear him sing, wi' a haun up tae his lug
Its funny how things come tae mind. Explain, I'm at a loss
Why should I think o' that auld man who sang at Govan Cross.

Why should I think of anything that happened auld lang syne?
Except that road doon memory lane is a favourite stroll o' mine.

Emigrant Shipyard worker. 1949.

MORRICE'S CORNER. 1937.

This popular and friendly newsagent/tobacconist shop was run by two Aberdonians and served the people of Govan, from the site of the present Subway, for over 40 years. Famous for its range of Dinky toys and Hornby train sets, its advertising window (above the bicycle) was always full – one of the reasons why the corner was extremely busy. This was also a favourite meeting place, particularly for first dates after a 'lumber fae the Towny'!

COMMERCIAL RESTAURANT. 1940.

'The inns and alehouses are so numerous as to form a great moral nuisance. Their pestiferous effects on the virtuous habits of the people are only too apparent'. Dr. Leishman. 1841.

Govanites, used to drinking in the traditionally spartan 'spit and sawdust' pub, received something of a culture shock (to which, in all fairness, they rapidly adjusted) in the shape of this fine example of Art Deco, complete with ground floor lounge and first floor restaurant. A touch of class which the good doctor would undoubtedly not have appreciated, but changed days indeed from the Ferrie Bot Inn! N.B. There was a teetotaller's entrance to the rear!

45

BEACON. 1939.

The last 'watering hole' for many before embarking on the long (last bus?) journey to the schemes. That many Govanites down the years agreed wholeheartedly with Bishop Leslie's comments on Govan's ale is amply evidenced in this (by no means exhaustive) list of notable twentieth century pubs:– Whitefield Bar, Arthur Mone's, Widdows, Three Ell Bar, Bells, Rose Queen, Dick Welsh's, Queen's, Castle, Albion, Albert, Kennedy's, Watson's, Rosshire, Govan Arms, Beacon, Jimmy Simpson's, Tower, Windsor, Stag, Lyceum, Weavers, Number One (first pub on Govan Rd after Linthouse), Number Two, Cosy Corner, Sheep's Heid, Boar's Heid, Roper's, Brechin's, Waverley, Harmony, Glen, Vital Spark, Gazelle, Kai Johansen's . . .

IRWINS. c. 1935.

A large drapery and outfitters store reflecting, along with the Co-op, what a busy shopping centre Govan was. One of the store's features was the delivery of customers' money to and from the cash desk via a metal canister propelled along over-head wires. In 1952, it became the Co-op Furniture and Fittings Emporium whose range of goods also included carpets, linoleum, jewellery, ironmongery, toys and fancy goods. One of the emporium's main attractions when it opened, since not too many families had their own TV, was its new radio and television department – complete with demonstration!

KINNING PARK CO-OPERATIVE SOCIETY LTD. c. 1934.

Originally the Fairfield Drapery Mansion House, the size of this store, set in the heart of the community, can be gauged from the fact that it occupied three levels – basement, street and 'one up' – and extended into three streets; Helen St, Langlands Rd, and Burleigh St. People came from 'a' the airts 'n pairts' for its annual sales, and it was also noted for its dairy and butcher shops. In 1952, it became the Glasgow South Co-operative Society Drapery Store. Amongst other large stores were Gillespies, Dands, Crosbies, Nicolls (with its menage) and Woolworths.

'THE ROAD TO GOVAN PIER'. Water Row. c. 1910.

'The oldest of existing records point to a ford . . . where the cross Ferry now plies. Indeed there is every probability that the road leading to it was a Roman way by which the legions of Hadrian crossed the river to establish their outlying station on Yorkhill'. (Brotchie).

49

PASSENGER FERRY, approaching Water Row. (1930). Service withdrawn in late 60s.

The wee toot oan the whustle tae start it oan its run,
An' the bumpin up the ferry steps, that gave the kiddies fun,
Tae think nae merr ah'll hear the shouts, as ma whistle gies a toot,
In tones o' disappointment: 'Aw, jings, the ferry's oot'.

But best tae think o' the racin' feet, the happy, merry din
The sparklin eyes, the merry shouts: 'Hurrah, the ferry's in'
Well freens, I guess ah've said enough, but partin's no sae merry,
But ah'll aye hae the fondest memories, o ma guid auld GOVAN FERRY.

VEHICULAR (or HORSE) FERRY, approaching Water Row. 1930.

First built in 1890, these carried cross river traffic till the opening of the Clyde Tunnel in 1965.

I'm skipper of the ferryboat,
I'm famous near and far,
I'll take your van, your baby's pram,
I'll take your motor car.
I'll get them over safely,
And I'll get them all across,
I'm captain of the ferry,
I'm Horatio McSherry,
I'm the pride of Govan Cross.

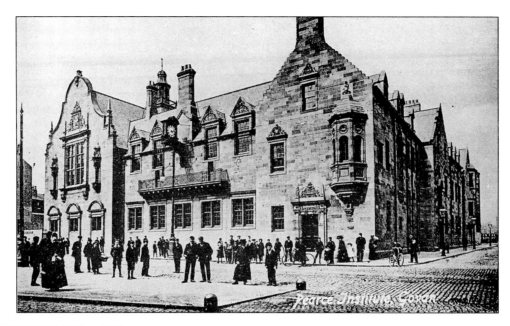

PEARCE INSTITUTE. c. 1905.

'This is a House of Friendship. This is a House of Service. For Families, For Lonely Folk. For the People of Govan. For the Strangers of the World. Welcome'. (On wall of Entrance).

A gift from Lady Pearce, the 'P.I.' was opened in 1904 with men's and women's reading rooms and clubs, a gymnasium, retiring room, cooking and laundry departments. In the 1920s, it was used as a games centre attached to the Kirk, and in the 1930s a club and general relief centre (Rev. – later Lord – George McLeod did much for the unemployed during the Depression). From 1939–45 it served as a war-time restaurant. The 'P.I.' survived a cash crisis in the 1970s and today is a busy educational and recreational centre – still with its own restaurant. The administrative headquarters of the Iona Community are based there.

THE BLACK MAN – Sir William Pearce (1833–88).

In 1869, Pearce became a partner in Fairfields, having been general manager in Robert Napier's firm. Although not an investor he had great business acumen. Govan became a Parliamentary Division in 1884 and a year later Pearce became its first MP (Conservative). In 1887, he was created a baronet for contributions to the navy and mercantile marine, and the statue was erected in 1894.

Govanites have always, literally, looked up to the statue, sometimes uncertainly and awkwardly, – especially since it occasionally seems to come to life – in the following case with criminal consequences!

Ah sweer ah saw the 'Black Man' nod, as ah went
stagg'rin by,
Sae up a look't an thocht it odd, and cursed him wi' a sigh.

An a' at once ah heard a sound, and thocht he's talkin'
noo,
Ah shoutit back, as he turned roond: 'Git stuffed fur ah'm
no fou'!

At Orkney Street, ah telt ma tale, tae men that cannae
laugh,
The serjeant widnae gie me bail, Nor the Baillie let me
aff!

(Courtesy: Bob McClement).

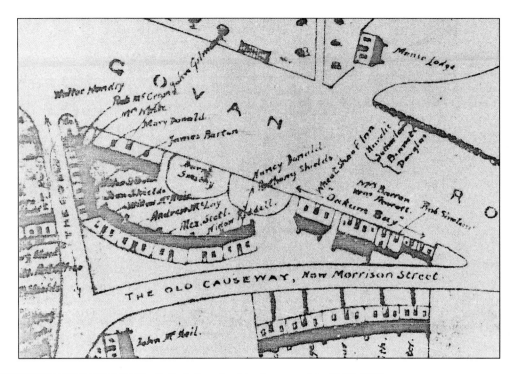

GOOD GOLLY MISS MOLLY! The Golly (after a local landowner – John Galt). 1837.

Although, through tradition and usage, the nickname came to refer to the area in and around Burleigh St (previously the Old Causeway, and Morrison St), the original area was at the bottom end of Harmony Row adjacent to St. Anthony's Primary School. Burleigh St was renamed after the famous war correspondent Bennet Burleigh, prospective Liberal MP for Govan (1885) who was narrowly defeated by Pearce. Oakum Bay was a row of thatched cottages, where Brechin's Bar now stands, occupied mainly by old people, employed preparing and teasing the oakum for caulking the seams of the wooden decks of ships.

HURLY BURLEIGH! Regal Tailors. Burleigh St. 1935.

Specialists for the well dressed man (he did occasionally change out of his overalls) and woman – and cheap at the price!
Just along this busy shopping street were, amongst others – Stewart the King's (later the Fifty Shilling) Tailor, Boots the
Chemist, Stewart the Butchers, Marshall's, Cherry's, Bayne & Ducket, and Greenlees (all shoe shops).

'THEIR NAMES LIVETH EVERMORE'. Remembrance Day at the War Memorial (Outside Old Parish Church). 1935.

Erected in 1922 in memory of the fallen of the Great War. Below, from the *Press*, are extracts from typical letters home from the Western Front:– 'We have an awful wilderness here and we are under fire all the time. There is no proper rest camp but we are cheerful and hopeful.' 'Would you be so kind as to see if any of your readers will be good enough to give me an old accordion as we are very lonely . . . There are a few Burndyke St lads . . . also from Holm St (Wanlock St). We are close on two years in this country . . . I always have the *Press* sent out. I remain one of Govan's own.' 'Imagine us walking for four days in the Elder Pond and you have a faint idea of what we suffer [in the trenches].'

THE GOOD OLD DAYS? McKechnie St, the 'Buroo'. c. 1935.

Govan was an almost exclusively working class area and its people, whose livelihood depended largely on shipbuilding, were particularly hard hit by unemployment and suffered severe poverty – particularly during the Depression. Many Govanites have long, painful memories of the dreaded and hated 'means test' –

Shabby clothes are worn by a',
An food at times is lent,
Bairnies then don't look sae braw,
Wives scrape tae pay the rent.
(*The Yairds*. J. F. Bell).

However, with our ramble over for now, let's recall, more fondly . . .

57

. . . All the Fun of the Fair . . .

The OLD GOVAN FAIR seems to have been in existence since the mid-twelfth century, and when the Govan Weavers Society was formed in 1756, with the primary purpose of considering 'the good and weel of the poor', it changed the fair from a market carnival to a trade display, adding by the first Friday of the following June, a procession led by a weaver carrying a sheep's head on a pole. (The sheep's heid symbolises pre-industrialised Govan when the wool industry was to the fore. It is one of the prized relics of the Society and lies on the table at the AGM).

The tradition lapsed in 1881 to be revived in 1920 by the OLD GOVAN CLUB (1914–71), which, apart from existing to recall the past and keep alive the spirit of Govan, also had a charitable aim. (Notable amongst their many fund-raising activities was the endowment of an operating theatre to the Elder Cottage Hospital). In 1926, the Govan Fair Committee emerged and in 1931 the first Fair Queen was crowned. In 1968, the Govan Fair Association took over and in 1977 the 'Fair' represented Strathclyde Regional Council at the Queen's Silver Jubilee celebrations.

The Old Govan Fair is still going strong, on the first Friday in June, and with the same charitable purpose as that of almost 340 years ago.

The atmosphere of the Fair in its heyday is perfectly captured by Margaret Thomson Davis in her novel *The Breadmakers*:–

'The marshalling point in Burghead Drive . . . was electrified by noise and colour. Spilling from both ends of the Drive were close on eighty decorated floats, motorvans and carts . . . Horses were stampering . . . flags were fluttering. The Boys' Brigade, cheeky pill box hats strapped tight under chins, were tippering drums.

Heavy-jowled mustachioed police pipers were concentrating, tartan pipes wailing . . . Jarring Jazz bands thumped a bouncy New Orleans beat. Further along in Elder Park another swarm of people waited impatiently for the Govan Fair Queen . . . The streets were awash with colour, Red, White and Blue Union Jacks . . . and the gold and red lion rampant of Scotland, swayed and flicked and cracked. After the police pipe band came the sheep's head held aloft, then the Navy band, then the Queen's landau and the motorcade of guests . . . Then came the decorated floats . . . bands and more bands until the whole of Govan rocked with sound. And tenements towered above the procession and tenants were a crush of faces and arms and hands at every window.'

(Not mentioned are the impromptu appearances and performances along the route by local merrymakers – some of whom ended their own celebrations with a night's rest at Orkney Street Police Station).

FAIR QUEEN, riding in state. 1950.

NOTORIANNI'S HORSE-DRAWN 'CAFE'. c. 1930.

'From a great part of the operative people in the village, temperance, it is much to be lamented, has not obtained a place amongst its cardinal virtues'. *Statistical Account* 1795.

The above statement, together with the presence of 77 public houses and 49 licenced grocers in the burgh by 1900, makes it surprising that cafes and ice-cream vans/wagons, coming in the wake of the Temperance movement, were not initially welcomed by officialdom. The real threat from what was seen as a 'pestilence and an insidious social evil' was of course to the Lord's Day observance since owners wished to trade on Sundays! Happily, these demoralising influences became a feature of tenement life e.g. Amy's, Sikis, Jean's, Plaza, Black Cat, Cafe de Luxe, Princess, Prego . . .

LOOKING EAST TO ELDERPARK ST. c. 1910.

Elder Park (formerly Fairfield Farm and known as the 'Govan Prairie') was gifted to the people of Govan in 1885 by Mrs. Isabella Elder in memory of her husband John. Amongst its more interesting bylaws were those stating that 'No person shall exercise, or break in a horse, ass or mule . . . wash any clothes in the lake nor place any dry clothes . . . beat, shake, clean mats or rugs . . . discharge any firearm or set off any balloon . . . read or recite any profane or obscene ballad . . . expose wounds or deformities inducing giving of alms'. Hardly worth a visit!

OLD MEN'S OUTING. 1952.

Govan people were always good to the older men of the 'Iron Burgh', and an annual bus trip was a feature of this generosity. Typical was the one above (to Barassie) where the beneficiaries were sent off with a crisp 10/- note, a 'wee hauf' and a bottle of beer. They did return! Note also the traditional wifies' pastime of windae hingin'!

ELDER PARK, Govan Rd entrance. 1955.

Conclusion of a draughts game between two Fairfields pensioners, perhaps the day after the bus run. Here the vanquished (with the hat and looking a little downcast) sportingly offers his congratulations to his conqueror –

'Well done, Pat. Ah've always said ah'm a good winner an' ah'm a good loser,' to be answered, equally graciously – 'Good on ye', John. It's jist a pity yir no' a good player!'

GOVAN'S OLD FIRM

BENS   'ANTS

Benburb (back row left to right): – Ferguson, Haddow, Forsyth, Bainbridge, Kyle, Montgomery. Front row (left to right): – Allan, McColl, Hawson, Thomson, Gilmour.

St. Anthony's (back row left to right): – Cloherty, Coogan, Higgins, Dyatt, Sheary, Bannan. Front row (left to right): - O'Donnell, McArthur, Bennet, Cassidy, Clark.

1953.

BENBURB JUNIORS FC (1900–   ).

Through a strong Protestant immigrant connection with Co. Tyrone, the club took its name from a village there and apparently played its earliest games in green and white! Govandale (near McKechnie St) and Gymnasium Park (Broomloan Rd) were home for Bens before the club settled at Tinto Park in 1932. Winners of the Scottish Cup in 1934 (3-1 v Bridgeton Waverley) and 1936 (1-0 v Yoker), they can also boast of winning two trophies on the same day – 31st May, 1924, when they won the Consolation Cup in the afternoon and the Kirkwood Shield in the evening. Most notable players to 'turn senior': Jimmy Mullan (Partick Thistle), Eric Smith, Johnny Divers, Mike Jackson, John Campbell (all Celtic!), Ron McKinnon (Rangers) and Jimmy Smith (Aberdeen).

ST. ANTHONY'S JUNIORS FC (1902–   ).

Born out of the Irish Catholic immigrant population, the club took its name from that of a local parish church. Their 'home' is Moore Park. League champions on six occasions, Ants just failed in 1919 to gain a unique place in Scottish Junior Football history when, having won the Glasgow Cup, Charity Cup, North Eastern Cup, Victory Cup and League Trophy, they lost to Glencairn in the Scottish Cup Final (0-1 after 1-1 draw). They also lost in the 1925 final (1-2 v Saltcoats Vics in a second replay). Most notable players to 'turn senior': John Gilchrist, Tommy McInally, Johnny McKay, Malky McDonald, Matt Lynch, Bobby Evans, and Willie O'Neill (all Celtic): most 'loyal' player – Frank McGrillan. 1951-69. 510 appearances.

THE CORPORATION WASH HOUSE, Clynder St. c. 1963.

Visits to the steamie (considered a soft option by tenement wash house users) were generally fitted around other house-hold chores (an aspect of family life for which the Govan man lacked enthusiasm) and, being escapism from domestic drudgery, were treated in part as social gatherings – an indoor Kittle Corner. Gossip abounded amongst the bleach, bub-bling carbolic soap, piping hot water, stalls and wringers, but it was hard work so:–

If yir granny complains o' her auld rheumatics,
Somethin' deep stirs in her memory attics,
Jist coont yirsel luckier than she's ever been,
When ye flick oan the switch o' yir washin' machine.
(Courtesy Jean Melville).

. . . as we finish with a cautionary tale of . . .

. . . THE GOVAN BILLIARD HALL.
(Tune – 'Maggie May')

Chorus:
O' don't staun an look aroon'
When the cues are upside doon.
An' the ba's are fleein' fast frae faur an' near,
For whether ye're tae blame
Ye'd be better aff at hame
When they're haunin' oot the stitches in yer ear.

Noo Govan is a busy place upon a Friday night,
An' the billiard rooms doon there are busy too,
An' many a strongly fancied lad's been rattled in a fight,
Jist for fiddlin' wi' the colours an' the cues.

'Twas on a certain Friday night, I went doon tae the saloon,
For I'd heard some fancy things aboot this dive,
So I moved up tae a table where two lads were tryin' hard
For to win three sets o' snooker oot o' five.

There were nearly three score Govan lads
Staunin' roon upon the tables lookin grim
For the wire had got aroon that wan lad wis two sets doon
An his chances noo were lookin' kind o' thin.

Noo the cool dab hand, the winnin' boy, wis lined up fur the [kill
He'd been stackin up the tricks in fives an' threes,
When the losin' wide-oh calls
As he joogles up the balls
'That's all, the gemme's a bogie if you please!'

Well ah didnae bother hingin' roon tae see how they got on,
Ah jist left them a' tae sort it oot themsels.
When the cues are upside doon in a Govan billiard room.
The safest place tae be is somewhere else!

(Words by Roddy McMillan.
Last verse by Adam McNaughton).

67

SELECTED FURTHER READING

Brennan, T., *Reshaping a City*, 1959.
Brotchie, T.C.F., *History of Govan*, 1905. (Reprinted 1938).
The Govan Press, 1878–1986.
Old Govan Club, *Transactions*, 1914–39.
Rountree, G., *A Govan Childhood: the 1930s*, 1993.
Simpson, J., *History of Govan*, 1985.

This material is available at the Mitchell and Elder Park Libraries.

ALSO IN THIS SERIES:
Cathcart and Environs, Jean Marshall, 1990.
Anderston as it was, David Glenday, 1992.
Old Cardonald had a Farm, John Innes, 1993.

On sale at any Glasgow City Library and bookshops.

POSTSCRIPT

Now is the hour . . . and the time to explain those omissions, of which I am only too aware. It's a 'racin' certainty' that some readers, chief among them more senior Govanites, will be armed with such constructive criticism as: – 'Magine no hivin' a foti i' the Lyceum . . . Ma auld school's no there . . . Iz that a' aboot Linthoose? . . . Missed oot the Fairfield Bar . . . Nae sign i' the Sufferin' General . . . Ah worked at the Shieldhall Factory – hit's no there . . . Diz he come fae Govan? (answer – Yes).

Well, assuming that no two people would have approached the subject in exactly the same manner and that, anyway, you can't please all of the people all of the time – ah dun ma best!

Hopefully, the reader has enjoyed this particular taste of Govan, perhaps with the appetite whetted for more, but at any rate I would be pleased to receive any comments, and to hear about any photographs and memories you may have. If so, please write to the author: c/o The Publications Board, The Mitchell Library, North Street, Glasgow G3 7DN.